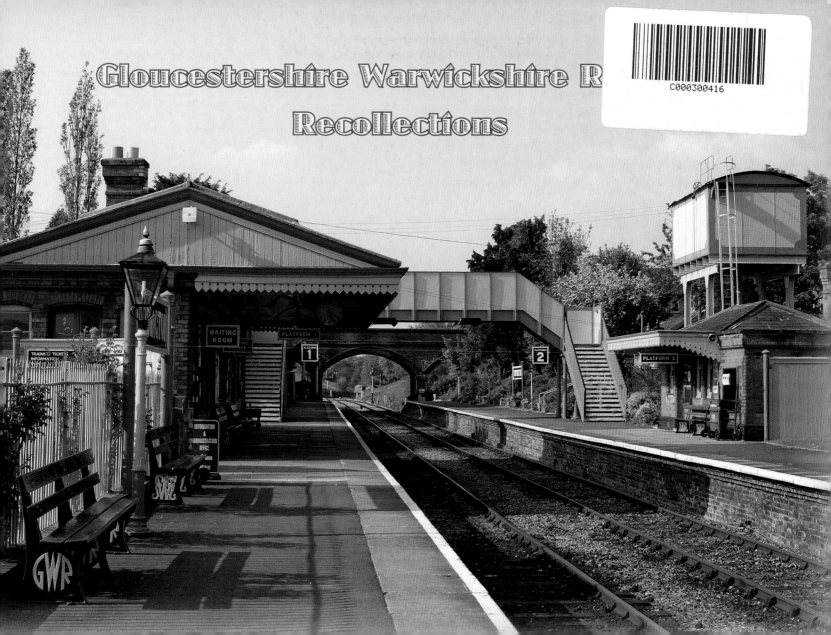

Gloucestershire Warwickshire Railway Recollections

Contents

Acknowledgments

Peter Townsend of Silver Link has brought his considerable enthusiasm, design and editing skills to bear on my images and text to good effect. The archive images were kindly supplied by Ian Crowder of the railway from the archives of Steam – The Museum of the Great Western Railway at Swindon; the Railway Archiving Trust at Toddington; photographer Tim Curr; and author and photographer John Stretton. This book was authorised and backed by the Gloucestershire Warwickshire Railway, and all the preservation images are my own work, many with the support and co-operation of the volunteers. I wish to record my appreciation of the tremendous work of volunteers past and present, from the early days of the 1980s to the present time, without whom there would be no railway to enjoy and photograph.

Malcolm Ranieri

First published in 2013

Printed and bound in Ceská Republika

About the author

Malcolm Edward Ranieri is a Warwickshire man, born and bred, and still lives in the county, so it was inevitable that when he decided to volunteer on a preserved railway it would be one that in the future may enter his home town of Stratford-upon-Avon. He has been a volunteer for 20 years or so on the Gloucestershire Warwickshire Railway, the last 15 as a Duty Station Master. Photography has been an all-consuming passion for 40 years, especially steam railways and vintage and classic transport. Malcolm became a Fellow of the Royal Photographic Society in 1998, and has since added the Masters award of the Photographic Alliance of Great Britain in 2000. Since retiring from local government in 1997 he has taken up photojournalism, reporting for magazines such as *Old Glory*. He had his first railway picture published in 1985, and since then many more in the pages of railway and transport journals. Malcolm has written eight published volumes to date: a history of traction engines; a previous photographic record of the Gloucestershire Warwickshire Railway; a classic modern traction volume; a classic commercial vehicle book; and four on traction engines for Silver Link Publishing ('Recollections' Nos 27 to 30).

Frontispiece: **TODDINGTON** This view of the Great Western Railway's Toddington station was taken in May 2012, looking towards Broadway and the roadbridge that takes the B4077 Stow-on-the-Wold road over the railway. The station was in a very dilapidated condition when taken over by the preservation group for restoration in 1981. The track was lifted in 1979, and before that the platforms were cut away to allow out-of-gauge freight trains to pass through. It is interesting to note that 100 years previously in 1913 passenger tickets issued amounted to 11,580, parcels forwarded 17,905, and general goods totalling 3,169 tons forwarded from the station. Of course, the Gloucestershire Warwickshire Railway now sells an equivalent number of passenger tickets, but alas no goods or parcels are forwarded.

British Library Cataloguing in Publication Data

A catalogue record for this book is available from the British Library.

© Malcolm Ranieri 2013

ISBN 978 1 85794 429 7

Silver Link Publishing Ltd
The Trundle
Ringstead Road
Great Addington
Kettering
Northants
NN14 4BW

Tel/Fax: 01536 330588
email: sales@nostalgiacollection.com
Website: www.nostalgiacollection.com

Introduction

I have been a supporter and volunteer on the Gloucestershire Warwickshire Railway for many years, and the images of the infrastructure, track layout, locomotives, operations, and, of course, the beautiful Cotswold scenery that form these 'Recollections' of the railway range from the 1990s to the present day, 20 years of progress.

I have seen the railway grow from just a few hundred yards of track in Toddington Yard in the 1980s, onward to Hayles Abbey Halt, then a rebuilt Winchcombe station, on to Gretton near the former Halt, gradually through the 1990s to Gotherington station, then the final push to Cheltenham Race Course station, which opened in 2003. Long-term plans include a return to Stratford-upon-Avon, though realistically Honeybourne, with its main-line connection, may be more achievable. Another possibility is a return to Cheltenham beyond the Race Course, and through Hunting Butts Tunnel; there are engineering problems to overcome, but the derelict trackbed is still in place up to a new supermarket across the former line. Already the railway operates to the former Laverton Halt over the spectacular Stanway Viaduct just north of Toddington station, and Broadway station is being rebuilt by a dedicated group. Once funds become available the track will be extended from Laverton Halt to Broadway station, and this popular tourist destination will once more be served by steam.

The railway, as I write, is just recovering from several embankment slips, one at Cheltenham Race Course, one at Gotherington, and a major one at the so-called 'Chicken Curve' embankment just to the north of Winchcombe station. This last slip severed the line from Toddington for two years and

cost in the region of £1 million to repair. Through all of this the railway has operated as best it could, with a truly magnificent effort from the volunteers. Winchcombe was the base for operations while the track was severed, with running to Cheltenham Race Course station by steam, and a diesel multiple unit (DMU) service at the Toddington end to Laverton Halt and Hayles Abbey. From the 2013 season the railway is once more whole and steam and diesel trains will operate the whole length of the current line, Cheltenham Race Course Station to Laverton Halt, a distance of some 13 miles, and can now look towards Broadway in the coming years. The railway aims to recreate a Great Western branch line, though in its heyday the route was an important main-line link from the Midlands to the South West, and the famous 'Cornishman' train ran over it from 1952 to 1962. The history of the line is as follows:

1859   A branch line from Stratford-upon-Avon to Honeybourne was opened by the Oxford, Worcester & Wolverhampton Railway (OWW), or the 'Old, Worse and Worse' as it was colloquially called.

circa 1900 The Great Western Railway (GWR) took over the OWW and obtained an Act for a high-speed line between Honeybourne and Cheltenham, officially named the Cheltenham & Honeybourne Line.

1906   The line was opened throughout on 1 August, entering Cheltenham at Lansdowne Junction.

1908   A line opened from Stratford-upon-Avon to

Tyseley, Birmingham, forming a through link for the GWR from the Midlands to the South West.

1960s   There was a gradual withdrawal of services up to 1969, then only diversions used the line, though freight continued to operate over it.

1976   A freight train derailed at Winchcombe, and the line closed south of Honeybourne on 1 November. A preservation society was founded to save the line from closure.

1979   The line was lifted by British Railways Western Region.

1981   The Gloucestershire Warwickshire Steam Railway was incorporated, and purchase of the line from Toddington to Cheltenham Race Course was completed.

1983   On 24 December a Light Railway Order was granted and a passenger service could begin.

1984   The full line from Broadway to Cheltenham was acquired in February. Operations commenced at Toddington.

The line runs through some glorious Cotswold scenery, bounded by hills and views of the Vale of Evesham and the distant Malverns. From Cheltenham Race Course station it heads north, passing under the Southam Road bridge at the bottom of the Race Course through shallow cuttings to Bishops Cleeve and the site of the former station, where trains on major race days were stabled; only the fir trees planted by the GWR remain to remind travellers. From Bishops Cleeve the line runs on an embankment to Gotherington station, which is in private hands and restored; the railway has built a Halt on the opposite platform. From Gotherington the line runs through Dixton cutting, under the minor road to Alstone village, and opposite the premises of the Prescott Hill Climb and the Bugatti Owners Club. From here the line is on embankments once more and an overbridge carries it across a road to the next destination of Gretton, where once stood a Halt near the railway bridge over the village road.

From Gretton, with views from the train towards the Malverns, the southern portal of Greet Tunnel is approached; at 693 yards, it is the second-longest in preservation. The line emerges from the northern portal into a broad-sided cutting, then enters Winchcombe station. The station is actually in the village of Greet, making it really 'Winchcombe Road' station, as the town is more than a mile away. The station has been rebuilt using the original Monmouth Troy station building. Of the original buildings only the goods shed, now the Carriage & Wagon Works, the weighbridge and staff accommodation remain, together with the extensive yards.

From Winchcombe station the line crosses the B4632 road, and over 'Chicken Curve' embankment, where the major slip severed the line to Toddington; the line did not re-open until two years later on 30 October 2012. From 'Chicken Curve' the line runs through the shallow cutting of the so-called 'Defford Straight' to the former Hayles Abbey Halt, though nothing remains of it. The Halt is a short distance from the National Trust and English Heritage ancient monument of Hailes Abbey (note the spelling), which was a victim of the Dissolution of the Monasteries in 1539. The Abbey was founded in 1245 and settled by Cistercian monks; next to the abbey ruins is the 1175-built Hailes Church.

From the Halt the line runs mainly on embankments, with views towards the Vale of Evesham, past the village of Didbrook and over the village minor road; from the train can be seen an original 'cruck' cottage (built with arched timbers) from the Middle Ages. The line then passes yards and buildings and enters Toddington station, the headquarters of the railway.

From Toddington the railway runs north under the B4077 roadbridge and into a cutting that leads to Stanway Viaduct, the major engineering feature on the line, 210 yards long and comprising 15 arches. The line then crosses embankments and passes through shallow cuttings, passing under the B4632 road to Broadway, to emerge at the current terminus at the former Laverton Halt; nothing remains of the Halt, but there is a run-round loop. Broadway is about 2 miles further on.

The railway was built by the GWR to a maximum gradient of 1 in 108, so there are no fierce gradients as the line climbs gently from Toddington to the summit at Gretton, then mostly downhill to Cheltenham. The Gloucestershire Warwickshire Railway headquarters are at Toddington station, where the locomotive sheds, yards and engineering facilities are based, and engines – steam and diesel – are stabled. Winchcombe station is the base for the Carriage & Wagon Works.

During its 30-year existence the Gloucestershire Warwickshire Railway has grown from a derelict former main line to its current status in the Top 10 of the country's preserved heritage railways – winning awards along the way such as the Ian Allan Heritage Railway of the Year in 2011 – and as a fine tourist attraction in the Cotswolds. It carries more than 60,000 passengers each year, and has plans to extend further than the current 13 miles of track, a tremendous achievement by a mainly volunteer workforce.

Malcolm Ranieri, January 2013

TODDINGTON A single-car diesel multiple unit (DMU) stands in Toddington station on 29 September 2011, operating the service at the north end of the line due to the slip at 'Chicken Curve', Winchcombe, which severed the track. The station opened in December 1904 as a railhead for fruit traffic, and there was a fruit packing shed in the goods yard, now demolished. The passenger service commenced in August 1906. The station closed to passenger traffic in March 1960, the goods yard followed in September 1967, and only freight trains and the occasional diversion used the line until closure in October 1976.

Toddington

Right: **TODDINGTON** There is something atmospheric and nostalgic about railways at night, especially with steam, and this image of locomotive No 4160 standing at Platform 1 shows not just the engine and freight wagon but the collections of suitcases, weighing machine, milk churns and porters' barrows, all of which add to the ambience of scene. No 4160 is a GWR Churchward and Collett '5101' Class 'Large Prairie' 2-6-2T, a medium-sized tank engine used for local and suburban services, and occasionally freight, all over the GWR system. The locomotive can usually be seen on the West Somerset Railway.

Left: **TODDINGTON** Another night image shows a steam locomotive standing at Platform 2. It is No 1450, a GWR '1400' Class 0-4-2T. Many of these locomotives were fitted with pull-and-push apparatus to work with auto-coaches specifically on the many branch lines of the company. The crew are taking a break on the platform next to the original waiting room. The railway hires in locomotives to work the services, though groups have and are restoring locomotives that also work on the line.

Turning the clock back...

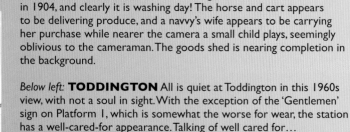

Below: **TODDINGTON** This is Toddington station under construction in 1904, and clearly it is washing day! The horse and cart appears to be delivering produce, and a navvy's wife appears to be carrying her purchase while nearer the camera a small child plays, seemingly oblivious to the cameraman. The goods shed is nearing completion in the background.

Below left: **TODDINGTON** All is quiet at Toddington in this 1960s view, with not a soul in sight. With the exception of the 'Gentlemen' sign on Platform 1, which is somewhat the worse for wear, the station has a well-cared-for appearance. Talking of well cared for...

Below: **TODDINGTON** No 7822 *Foxcote Manor* runs through Toddington station with a set of maroon coaches in March 2002. These GWR Collett '7800' Class 4-6-0s, designed in 1938, were built for use on passenger and freight trains over weight-restricted lines such as those of the former Cambrian Railways. As a lad I can remember a trip to the seaside at Aberystwyth over the severe gradients of the Central Wales line, especially at Talerddig, being pulled by a 'Manor', an experience I won't forget with its impressive performance.

Left: **TODDINGTON** No 1450 and two auto-coaches wait for their next turn of duty in Toddington station in June 2010. Locomotives fitted for this type of working on GWR branch lines were often placed in the centre between the two coaches, for extra passenger seating. Coach No W231 is in BR carmine and cream livery, while the second coach is in GWR chocolate and cream livery.

Below left: **TODDINGTON** While the 'Chicken Curve' embankment slip caused the line to be severed, Santa trains were run from each end of the line. At the north end a two-car DMU was used, with Santa on board; on 17 December 2011 Santa and a satisfied customer stand by the DMU. The railway derives a considerable percentage of its yearly income from Santa trains.

Below: **TODDINGTON** This view of Toddington station is looking south towards Cheltenham from the B4077 roadbridge.

Above: **TODDINGTON** station is seen from the drive to the car park and yards, a view that has probably not changed much in the century since it was built.

Top right: **TODDINGTON** The re-opening of the railway after the 'Chicken Curve' embankment slip repairs had been completed took place on 30 October 2012. The first train for two years to steam through from Toddington to Winchcombe and beyond was hauled by No 7903 *Foremarke Hall*, quite fittingly as this locomotive has done sterling service at the railway over the past few years. No 7903 carries the 'Cheltenham Spa Express' headboard; this passenger train was operated by the GWR in the 1930s from Paddington, London, to Cheltenham Spa, and was often called the 'Cheltenham Flyer'.

Left: **TODDINGTON** The Gloucestershire Warwickshire Railway has its own dedicated fire crew and one of the vehicles they operate is this 1969 Ford fire engine, which is based at Toddington station.

Left: **TODDINGTON** The railway attracts classic vehicles of all kinds, and each year there are several planned classic vehicle days in the events diary. However, this iconic 1950 Bedford OB coach has brought a party to travel on the train on 19 October 2011, and is seen about to depart. In the background is the replica GWR 7-foot-gauge locomotive *Iron Duke*, which was built by the Great Western Society at Didcot.

Above: **TODDINGTON** As with the Bedford OB, an unannounced visit was made to the railway on 21 July 2010 by the Steam Car Club of Great Britain, and here with the replica *Iron Duke* are three Stanley Steam Cars from the early 1900s.

Right: **TODDINGTON** The Scammell Mechanical Horse was a common sight at many railway stations from the 1930s to the 1960s; it replaced the horse and cart, hence the name, and was a common carrier to and from the local station. This particular Scammell Scarab is owned by a member of the railway and is stored at Toddington; it was not originally a railway company vehicle, but is restored and painted in a Southern Railway livery.

Above left: **TODDINGTON** In an interesting cameo in Toddington car park on 3 June 2010, the steam locomotive on display is No 5051 *Earl Bathurst*, one of the GWR Collett 'Castle' Class 4-6-0 main-line express locomotives, and the lorry drawn up alongside is a 1955 Bristol HG6L, a British Road Services vehicle, and the two drivers appear to be swapping stories.

Above: **TODDINGTON** The original GWR goods shed at Toddington is now a machining facility and operations office.

Left: **TODDINGTON** These are the yards at Toddington in January 2013, with the engine sheds in the background. The running line is on the extreme right of the image.

Left: **TODDINGTON** This is a December departure from Platform 1 at Toddington taken from the pedestrian overbridge – all steam and spectacle and heavy frost on the rails. A second Santa train is waiting in Platform 2.

Below: **TODDINGTON** Steam locomotive No 2857 is seen at the water tower at the end of the platforms at Toddington, heading a demonstration freight train on 19 October 1992. The original GWR water tower was on Platform 2, and has now been restored to its correct position, though not yet operational. No 2857 is a Churchward '28XX' Class 2-8-0 heavy freight engine, the main mover of freight on the GWR up to nationalisation in 1948.

Above left: **TODDINGTON** Departing from Toddington station on 23 August 2010 is 8F No 45160, (no, not a 'Black 5' but the number allocated by Turkish State Railways) or No 8274 (LMS number) – both numbers are being carried in this shot. Several hundred Stanier 2-8-0 freight engines were built for the London Midland & Scottish Railway (LMS), this one having been shipped to Turkey by the War Department during the Second World War. Repatriated from there by the Churchill 8F Society in 1989, No 45160 was restored over the following 20 years. These relatively modern steam engines worked until the end of steam on British Railways. The train is the railway's dining special, 'Elegant Excursions', and in the station is a Class 37 diesel locomotive waiting to take out the next service train.

Above: **STANWAY HALL** For many years the railway ran a Steam & Vintage Fair at Toddington and, for one year, at Cheltenham, and among other classic machinery several steam traction engines took part. Most years a road run to nearby Stanway Hall took place. Seen here in the courtyard of the Hall in October 2003 is an 1889 Hornsby of Grantham traction engine, works number 6557, named *Maggie*, and behind it is an 1886 Marshall of Gainsborough traction engine, works number 14421, named *Sparks*.

Left: **TODDINGTON** Another form of departure from Toddington station, on the B4077 just outside the station entrance, is a 1960 Daimler CVG6DD with a Weymann body. It was No 112 in the Swindon fleet, and is now privately owned. It is taking part in the Classic Bus Rally on 22 July 2012.

Didbrook Embankment

Above: **TODDINGTON** No 5199 departs from Toddington station on 4 May 2004 and passes the signal box that controls the station and yards. The locomotive is a GWR Class '51XX' 2-6-2T standard express passenger tank engine, and the signal box is original, although restored in 1984 with a new signal frame from Earlswood Lakes on the North Warwickshire line.

Above right: **DIDBROOK EMBANKMENT** On 3 November 2001 No 92203 is pulling a demonstration freight train at Didbrook. The engine belongs to David Shepherd, the renowned artist, and he named it *Black Prince*; for some years it was resident at the railway, but is now on the North Norfolk Railway. No 92203 is a member of the 9F Class of 2-10-0s, the final steam design by BR, and some say the best; built from 1954 to 1960, this example was withdrawn in 1967.

Right: **DIDBROOK EMBANKMENT** On 31 May 2007 visiting engine *Wadebridge* is seen on Didbrook Embankment approaching the site of Hayles Abbey Halt. *Wadebridge* is a Southern Railway (SR) Bulleid 'West Country' 'light Pacific', numbered 21C107 in SR days and in BR days 34007, the number carried here.

DIDBROOK EMBANKMENT The railway has a number of heritage diesel locomotives in its fleet, most owned by private individuals or groups, and they are used on certain timetables between steam workings; there are also dedicated diesel working days. Here on 22 August 2010 a Class 37 heads towards Toddington. These diesel-electric locomotives were built by English Electric at Vulcan Foundry and Robert Stephenson & Hawthorns between 1960 and 1965; 45 are preserved and a few still work in private ownership on the main line.

DIDBROOK EMBANKMENT In the misty conditions of 12 December 2010 No 5542 is seen at Didbrook on a Santa Special. No 5542 is a GWR '45XX' Class 2-6-2T 'Light Prairie' passenger tank engine built in 1928 for cross-country and branch-line work. It has seen regular use on the line but can usually be seen on the West Somerset Railway.

Hayles Abbey Halt

Right: **HAYLES ABBEY HALT** Turning the clock back once more, here we see Hayles Abbey Halt before the demolition crew swept it away.

Below: **HAYLES ABBEY HALT** This is the site of the Halt today (the village is actually spelled Hailes). It was opened by the GWR on 24 September 1928 and closed on 7 March 1960. It was constructed of two facing platforms built with used wooden sleepers, with an iron corrugated waiting shelter on each platform, accessed by footpaths from the adjacent minor road. It was opened to serve the museum at Hailes Abbey, and in the 1930s was served by six daily railmotors. The train seen here on 4 April 1992 is hauled by No 2857, a GWR heavy freight engine of the same class as Nos 2807 and 3803.

Below right: **HAYLES ABBEY HALT** On 30 August 1997 No 45596 *Bahamas* is approaching Hayles Abbey Halt with a passenger train. The locomotive is an LMS 'Jubilee' Class 4-6-0, one of the last of Sir William Stanier's express passenger locomotives built in the 1930s. Hired in by the railway, it has also seen main-line use on charter specials.

Above: **HAYLES ABBEY HALT** No 2807 approaches the Halt with a Santa Special on 12 December 2010. The locomotive is a GWR Churchward '28XX' Class 2-8-0 standard heavy freight engine; restored by the Cotswold Steam Preservation Group, it is a regular engine on the railway.

Below: **HAYLES ABBEY HALT** At the same position but heading towards Toddington is a three-car DMU set forming a Santa Special train on 17 December 2011.

Right: **HAYLES ABBEY HALT** Having just crossed Didbrook Embankment, No 3803 approaches Hayles Abbey Halt on 17 June 2010. This engine was hired in from Didcot Railway Centre and is a similar locomotive to Nos 2807 and 2857, both seen earlier, being a GWR heavy freight engine, although here being used on a passenger train.

Right: **HAYLES ABBEY HALT** On 21 October 1996 No 4920 *Dumbleton Hall*, with a demonstration freight train, works away from the site of Hayles Abbey Halt towards Winchcombe. No 4920 is a GWR Collett 'Hall' Class 4-6-0 standard mixed-traffic engine, versatile locomotives that worked all over the GWR system. The engine is named after a stately home local to the railway, Dumbleton being a village only a few miles away; Dumbleton Hall itself is now a hotel.

Left: **DEFFORD STRAIGHT** No 5199 is seen on 4 May 2004 on the so-called 'Defford Straight' between Hayles Abbey and Winchcombe.

Lower left: **DEFFORD STRAIGHT** No 45596 *Bahamas* is also seen on the 'Defford Straight', on 30 August 1997.

Below: **DEFFORD STRAIGHT** The village of Greet and Winchcombe station and its yards are spread out behind the Santa Special train hauled by David Shepherd's 9F No 92203 *Black Prince* on 17 December 2006 as it heads towards Toddington. The image was taken from Salters Hill, 263 feet above sea level, looking down on the village and railway; the Cotswold Way, a long-distance path, crosses the hillside.

Below: **CHICKEN CURVE** This is the so-called 'Chicken Curve', named because a chicken farm was sited just below the embankment, although the buildings are no longer in use as such. This was where an embankment slip severed the railway for two years. In happier times, on 19 October 1993, locomotive No 46521 hauls a demonstration freight train around the curve, watched by grazing sheep; this piece of land actually belongs to the railway. No 46521 is an LMS H. G. Ivatt Class '2' 2-6-0 standard light engine – often nicknamed 'Mickey Mouse' – for use on cross-country lines with weight restrictions.

Above: **CHICKEN CURVE** On 18 October 1998 No 4277 is seen rounding the curve with a passenger train bound for Toddington. No 4277 is a GWR Churchward 2-8-0T heavy tank engine that was used for short-distance mineral traffic; many were seen in the South Wales coalfield in steam days.

Left: **CHICKEN CURVE** No 1450 is seen at 'Chicken Curve' on 18 October 1998, taking a local train from Winchcombe to Toddington.

Below: **CHICKEN CURVE** This is the train that the Gloucestershire Warwickshire Railway waited two years to see. The re-opening of the repaired 'Chicken Curve' took place on 30 October 2012, and No 7903 *Foremarke Hall*, carrying the 'Cheltenham Spa Express' headboard, had the honour of taking the first passenger train over the embankment and into Winchcombe station.

Winchcombe

WINCHCOMBE On 25 May 2003 No 6412 takes a passenger train out of Winchcombe station towards Toddington. On the left is the signal box, and on the right part of the extensive yards, holding much of the railway's rolling stock. No 6412 is a GWR '57XX' Class 'all-purpose' 0-6-0 pannier tank locomotive, one of 863 engines of this popular and ubiquitous locomotive to have been built.

WINCHCOMBE No 7903 *Foremarke Hall* runs through Winchcombe station. It should really be called 'Winchcombe Road', as the town centre is more than a mile away, and the station is in the village of Greet. Seen here is the original Monmouth Troy station building, taken down and re-erected brick by brick on the site of the demolished Winchcombe station. Much extra building work has taken place since, including a waiting room on Platform 2 and a re-erected pedestrian bridge, all in keeping with the original layout. The GWR opened the station in 1905 and BR Western Region closed it in 1960. Receipts from 1913 show that 21,824 passengers were carried and 11,828 tons of goods, probably mostly agricultural. After closure, the only buildings to remain were the weighbridge and office, still a popular feature, the goods shed, now the Carriage & Wagon Works, residential accommodation, now a bed & breakfast establishment, and some of the yards. The current signal box was sourced from Hall Green on the North Warwickshire line, and the 37-lever frame came from Honeybourne West Loop box.

WINCHCOMBE On 11 November 2012 the DMU at Platform 2 waiting to depart for Toddington is passed by No 7903 *Foremarke Hall*, running tender-first into Platform 1 from Cheltenham. Prior to the slip at 'Chicken Curve', Winchcombe personified a quiet branch-line station, with a few passengers coming and going and passing trains from each end of the line. After the slip, it became the terminus and was a busy station, very much like a century before, and such were the numbers attending that a café was built in the waiting room, which has proved popular. Now that Toddington station is the major station once again it will be interesting to see how Winchcombe is affected.

Right: **WINCHCOMBE** The railway works hard to illustrate a GWR branch line, and little touches on the stations like these fire buckets at Winchcombe really help to set the scene.

Below: **WINCHCOMBE** station is seen from the pedestrian footbridge looking towards Platform 1 in January 2013.

Right: **WINCHCOMBE** This is the station from Platform 1, also in January 2013. At the end of the building is the Station Master's Office and Booking Office.

Above: **WINCHCOMBE** No 7903 *Foremarke Hall* waits at Platform 2 on 20 October 2011, seen from the road overbridge that takes the B4078 to Winchcombe.

Right: **WINCHCOMBE** The former goods shed in the yard at Winchcombe station is now the railway's Carriage & Wagon Works.

WINCHCOMBE
No 7903 *Foremarke Hall* departs from Winchcombe for Cheltenham in a cloud of steam on 20 October 2011.

Right: **WINCHCOMBE**
The railway will be holding a 'Wartime in the Cotswolds' event in April 2013, and a preview event was held at Winchcombe station on 22 July 2012, as seen in this sequence of pictures. In the first, Airborne Regiment soldiers guard Winchcombe station.

Far right: **WINCHCOMBE**
Soldiers guard Winchcombe signal box.

Below: **WINCHCOMBE**
Soldiers take their leave at Cheltenham Race Course station.

Below: **WINCHCOMBE** A mortar camp is set up behind Platform 2.

Turning the clock back...

Top and above: **WINCHCOMBE** The top picture shows Winchcombe station under construction in 1904. Almost 60 years later the station has settled into its environs, and the pine trees, characteristic of a number of GWR stations, are now well established.

Above right: **WINCHCOMBE** 'Black 5' No 44777 approaches Winchcombe round 'Chicken Curve' on 12 June 1965 with the Birmingham (Snow Hill) to Bath Green Park leg of the Warwickshire Railway Society's 'Somerset & Dorset Joint & Eastleigh Tour'. The outward journey to Eastleigh Works was via Oxford. Even at this late stage in its working life No 44777 managed to pass through Race Course station at a respectable 78mph!

Above left: **WINCHCOMBE** No 3803 departs from Winchcombe station on 17 June 2010, passing under the B4078 roadbridge and a blanket of cow parsley on the cutting side.

Above: **WINCHCOMBE** No 7903 *Foremarke Hall* leaves Winchcombe on 11 March 2012 and approaches the signal gantry sited in the wide cutting.

Left: **WINCHCOMBE** *Foremarke Hall* is seen again departing from Winchcombe for Cheltenham on 20 October 2011, and proceeds up the wide cutting on the approaches to Greet Tunnel.

Greet Tunnel

Right: **GREET TUNNEL** No 65462 and a demonstration freight are seen in Winchcombe cutting on the approaches to Greet Tunnel on 17 November 2007. The locomotive is a Great Eastern Railway Class 'J15' 0-6-0 built prior to the First World War and a 'maid of all work' used on passenger and freight trains, especially pick-up goods, in the Eastern counties. The GER was absorbed into the London & North Eastern Railway in 1923.

Left: **GREET TUNNEL** No 46521, heading a demonstration freight, thunders out of the northern portal of Greet Tunnel heading for Winchcombe station on 19 October 1993.

Below: **GREET TUNNEL** No 7903 *Foremarke Hall* heads into the northern portal of Greet Tunnel (sometimes called Winchcombe Tunnel for obvious reasons) on 11 March 2012. The tunnel is 693 yards long and is the second-longest in preservation.

GREET TUNNEL No 7903 *Foremarke Hall* leaves the southern portal of Greet Tunnel on 21 April 2012.

GREET TUNNEL 8F 2-8-0 No 8274 heads towards the southern portal on 4 June 2012.

Opposite above: **GREET TUNNEL** No 2807 enters the wide cutting outside the southern portal on 13 November 2011. The views from here are spectacular – the Malverns can be seen on a clear day. Behind the train can be seen Dixton Hill (164 feet) and, behind that, Oxenton Hill at 223 feet.

Opposite below: **GREET TUNNEL** No 7903 *Foremarke Hall* runs through the wide cutting and heads for Gretton on 11 November 2012.

Above: **GREET TUNNEL** No 2807 rounds the curve and enters the wide cutting near the southern portal on 13 November 2011.

Below: **GREET TUNNEL** 8F No 8274 heads towards the southern portal on 27 September 2012. Beyond the train is the village of Gretton, and before the overbridge on the main village road is the site of Gretton Halt, nothing of which now remains. The Halt opened in August 1906 and consisted of two facing 100 foot-long wooden trellis platforms, each of which carried a 'pagoda'-style passenger shelter. In its first year the Halt was served by seven weekday railmotor services; it closed in March 1960.

Above: **FAR STANLEY** No 7903 *Foremarke Hall* is seen at Far Stanley on 19 October 2011. There are views here across to the Vale of Evesham. The author and preservationist L. T. C. (Tom) Rolt, founder of the Inland Waterways Association and the Talyllyn Railway Preservation Society, lived near here at Stanley Pontlarge, a hamlet to the right of the picture, and talks about the railway in his books.

Above: **FAR STANLEY** *Foremarke Hall* is seen again from the hillside above Far Stanley village, near an ancient drover's road, on 10 March 2012.

Below: **DIXTON CUTTING** No 7903 approaches Dixton Cutting and is about to cross the B4632 road to Gotherington on 11 November 2012.

Below: **DIXTON CUTTING** Class 73 electro-diesel locomotive No 73129, resident on the railway, approaches Dixton cutting with a passenger train on 6 May 2012. The Class 73s were able to operate on electrified third rail lines (as on the Southern Region) but had an on-board diesel engine for non-electrified lines. They were built between 1962 and 1967 by BR Eastleigh and English Electric at Vulcan Foundry, and a few still work on the main line.

Above: **DIXTON CUTTING**
8F No 8274 runs through Dixton Cutting on 27 September 2012. A short distance away from the railway is Prescott Hill Climb and the Bugatti Owners Club museum.

Above right: **DIXTON CUTTING**
No 4277 roars through Dixton Cutting on 8 March 1998.

Above: **DIXTON CUTTING**
No 2807 bursts through the road overbridge that carries a minor road to the village of Alstone, and enters Dixton Cutting on 19 September 2012.

Above: **DIXTON CUTTING** Heading towards Gotherington station in Dixton Cutting on 25 September 2005 is a train double-headed by diesel locomotives Nos 56013 and 73129. No 56013 was built by Electropoture, Romania, in the late 1970s, mainly for freight work; five of these locomotives are preserved.

Gotherington

Above: **GOTHERINGTON** No 9466 approaches the roadbridge, having just departed from Gotherington station on 4 June 2010. No 9466 is a GWR Class '94XX' 0-6-0PT built in 1947 at Swindon Works.

Above right: **GOTHERINGTON** 8F No 8274 departs from Gotherington station on 3 October 2012 and runs past the avenue of fir trees planted by the GWR. Gotherington station building has been restored and is a private residence; a halt shelter has been built by the railway on the opposite platform. The station opened in June 1906, eventually being renamed Gotherington Halt in 1940, and closed in June 1955, the first to close on the line. The railway has added a passing loop, and a signal box has been erected in recent times.

Right: **GOTHERINGTON** The 8F is seen again on the same day in the same position as the picture above, but from the vantage point of Nottingham Hill, 279 feet above sea level, and looking towards Dixton Hill at 164 feet.

Above: **GOTHERINGTON** No 7903 *Foremarke Hall* departs from Gotherington station on 1 June 2007.

Above right: **GOTHERINGTON** No 2807 is also seen at Gotherington station, on 22 April 2011. The station is the subject of a recently published book, No 14 in the 'Recollections' series, by the owner, Bryan Nicholls.

Right: **GOTHERINGTON** *Foremarke Hall* leaves Gotherington and passes the loop heading for Bishops Cleeve on 11 November 2012. On the left can be seen some of the railwayana and other memorabilia collected and erected by the station's current owner.

Below: **GOTHERINGTON** Heading towards the station at Manor Lane is No 3440 *City of Truro* with a short train of carmine and cream coaches on 26 November 2006. No 3440 is part of the collection of the National Railway Museum at York, and was stabled and used at the Gloucestershire Warwickshire Railway for some years. The locomotive is a GWR Dean 4-4-0 express passenger engine built in 1903, originally numbered 3717, and achieved worldwide fame in 1905 at the head of a parcels train as the first railway engine to attain 100mph, though there

has always been some doubt about the claim. However, there is no denying that this handsome GWR engine attracts enthusiasts wherever she goes, and was very popular at the railway.

Right: **GOTHERINGTON** *Foremarke Hall* is seen just beyond the passing loop at Gotherington at Manor Lane, named after the nearby Manor Farm, on 11 November 2012.

Right: **GOTHERINGTON** No 2807 picks up the last of the winter light at Manor Lane on a Santa Special from Cheltenham to Winchcombe on 17 December 2011.

Below: **GOTHERINGTON** No 92203 *Black Prince* heads towards Gotherington on 26 November 2006, also catching the late-winter backlighting.

Bottom: **GOTHERINGTON** No 7903 *Foremarke Hall* is seen at Manor Lane on 11 March 2012, having just left the passing loop at Gotherington station, and heads south. Nottingham Hill is behind the train.

Right: **GOTHERINGTON**
No 92203 *Black Prince* heads towards Gotherington station at Manor Lane, just out of Bishops Cleeve, with the Cleeve Hill range in the background. These hills top out at 330 feet at their highest point.

Bishops Cleeve

Below left: **BISHOPS CLEEVE** 8F No 8274 passes the site of Bishops Cleeve station, in a photograph taken from the summit of Cleeve Hill on 1 January 2013 – the whole of Bishops Cleeve and Woodmancote are in view. There is nothing left of Bishops Cleeve station apart from the fir trees planted by the GWR. The station was opened in 1906 and closed in March 1960; it is difficult to imagine now, but it had waiting/booking offices on both platforms, a goods shed, weighbridge, cattle pens, sidings and a signal box. It is interesting to note that in 1913 14,239 passenger tickets were sold and 1,932 parcels were forwarded, and in the 1930s there was a staff of five – how times have changed.

Below: **WOODMANCOTE** Nos 3205 and 7903 double-head through Woodmancote on 11 September 2004. No 3205 is a GWR Collett '2251' Class 0-6-0 built in 1946. These engines used to regularly work services to and from Stratford-upon-Avon.

Cheltenham Race Course

Right: **CHELTENHAM RACE COURSE** 8F No 8274 departs from the station on 1 January 2013; the photograph was taken from Cleeve Hill overlooking the Racecourse.

Below: **CHELTENHAM RACE COURSE** No 4936 *Kinlet Hall* is at Southam Road overbridge, which can be seen in the background, at the bottom of the Racecourse on 2 May 2005. No 4936 is a sister locomotive to No 7903, and has seen main-line work from her base at Tyseley.

Below right: **CHELTENHAM RACE COURSE** No 7903 *Foremarke Hall* departs from the station at Southam Road overbridge on 28 March 2005.

Turning the clock back...

CHELTENHAM RACE COURSE It is 25 June 1965 and 9F No 92224 heads north through Cheltenham Race Course station with a long train of coal empties. The closed station makes an interesting comparison with the following image – the trees have certainly stood the test of time. Sadly No 92224, built in 1958, fared less well, being withdrawn in September 1967 and cut up the following year.

CHELTENHAM RACE COURSE No 30925 *Cheltenham* – actually sister locomotive *Repton* – runs through Cheltenham Race Course station. The station opened in March 1912 and was used mainly on race days, closure taking place in February 1964. It is unusual in that the Booking Office is at a higher level than the track, though the Gloucestershire Warwickshire Railway has built a waiting room, offices and toilets, and a water tower on Platform 1, and a signal box at the end of the platforms. Platform 2 remains unrestored, though there are plans to rectify this. Race Course is the current terminus, but beyond it in GWR days was, for a short while, Cheltenham High Street Halt, closed in 1917, then Cheltenham St James station. No 30925, renumbered from 928 as *Cheltenham*, is a Maunsell Southern Railway 4-4-0 'Schools' Class locomotive.

Left:
CHELTENHAM RACE COURSE
This view of the station from the Racecourse on 15 January 2013 shows that the Booking Office building has now been restored from a derelict condition by the local Cheltenham group; it was originally prefabricated at the GWR's Swindon Works.

Above: **CHELTENHAM RACE COURSE**
This view from Platform 1 is looking under the main A435 Cheltenham road towards Hunting Butts Tunnel on 15 January 2013. A run-round loop extends towards the tunnel and some stock is stored near the tunnel mouth.

Left: **CHELTENHAM RACE COURSE** The view in the opposite direction towards Bishops Cleeve on the same day shows the signals and signal box.

Left: **TODDINGTON** Now we take a look at the extension from Toddington northwards towards Broadway. 8F No 45160, with a passenger train, enters Toddington station through the steep-sided cutting from Stanway Viaduct on 28 November 2010.

Below: **TODDINGTON** The 8F, now running as No 8470, enters Toddington station with a demonstration freight train on 3 June 2010, seen from the B4077 Stow-on-the-Wold road.

Above: **STANWAY VIADUCT** No 3440 *City of Truro* heads a passenger train over the impressive viaduct on 26 April 2010. With 15 arches and a length of 210 yards, it is the largest anywhere on a UK heritage railway.

Left: **STANWAY VIADUCT** In contrast to the iconic *City of Truro*, No 5542 and an auto-coach cross the viaduct and head for Toddington on 4 June 2010.

Above: **LAVERTON** This is the current end of the line, and the run-round loop at the site of the former Laverton Halt is seen here on 16 October 2012. Located about half a mile from the village, the Halt opened in August 1905 and closed in March 1960. It was constructed in the same manner as the other halts on the line, with two facing platforms of wooden sleepers and 'pagoda'-style waiting rooms.

Above right: **LAVERTON** This is where the line finally terminates. The view is looking towards Broadway, about 2 miles north.

Right: **LAVERTON** A two-car DMU approaches the B4632 Broadway to Toddington roadbridge bound for Laverton on 3 October 2012.

Broadway

Above: **BROADWAY** This is the current position at the station, being restored and rebuilt by the local Broadway Area Group from a completely derelict site apart from the remaining platform edges. The station was opened in October 1904 and closed to passengers in March 1960; it is located on the edge of the town next to the A44 roadbridge.

Left: **BROADWAY** Passengers are gathering for the next departure, and extension work is taking place in this early-1900s view, which illustrates the challenge ahead. In 1913 17,440 passenger tickets were issued, 17,075 parcels handled, and 1,139 tons of general goods forwarded. Between the wars there was a staff of up to ten, who were required to handle a lot of fruit and vegetable traffic besides the passengers.

Below: **BROADWAY** In 1960 the station looks to be in a good state of repair and general all-round tidiness as Collett '1400' Class 0-4-0 No 1424 waits to depart with a push-pull service towards Honeybourne Junction, before which it will call at Willersey Halt and Weston-sub-Edge.

The trackbed back to Honeybourne is basically still in situ, and during the recent re-doubling of the Cotswold Line by Network Rail the layout at Honeybourne has been designed to facilitate a return of tracks to the erstwhile island platform – a tantalising prospect for the years ahead!

Left: **BROADWAY** Looking towards Honeybourne in early 2013, the restoration work at the station is well under way with the platform edges in place, complete with newly painted white edging!

Index of locomotives

In the same series:

Railways & Recollections
GOTHERINGTON STATION By Brian Nicholls

This story is unusual in that it documents not only the complete restoration and reinstatement of both platforms at a former Great Western Railway country station but also the building of a brand new standard-gauge running line with its own private station and rolling stock. Even more remarkable is the fact that all of this was achieved on a shoestring budget and by the sheer hard toil and dedication of a tiny workforce.

Although a private residence, the best views and probably the best way of assessing the scale of the project is to take a ride on the Gloucestershire Warwickshire Railway between Cheltenham and Winchcombe. The summer floral displays are not to be missed, and you may even find yourself running parallel to one or other of the various items of weird and wonderful rolling stock!